I0067361

Buyers, Sellers, Agents, Business Coaching Prospects
call me with any and all questions at 508-726-3492.

—Kyle Seyboth

Being the Best Version of Yourself

Live to Your Fullest Potential as a Real Estate Agent

Kyle Seyboth

THiNKaha®

An Actionable Business Journal

E-mail: info@thinkaha.com
20660 Stevens Creek Blvd., Suite 210
Cupertino, CA 95014

Copyright © 2022, Kyle Seyboth

All rights reserved. No part of this book shall be reproduced, stored in a retrieval system, or transmitted by any means other than through the AHAthat platform or with the same attribution shown in AHAthat without written permission from the publisher.

Please go to
https://aha.pub/BestVersionOfYourself
to read this AHAbook and to share the
individual AHA messages that resonate with you.

Published by THiNKaha®
20660 Stevens Creek Blvd., Suite 210,
Cupertino, CA 95014
https://thinkaha.com
E-mail: info@thinkaha.com

First Printing: June 2022
Hardcover ISBN: 978-1-61699-396-2   1-61699-396-0
Paperback ISBN: 978-1-61699-395-5   1-61699-395-2
eBook ISBN: 978-1-61699-394-8   1-61699-394-4
Place of Publication: Silicon Valley, California, USA
Paperback Library of Congress Number: 2022900009

Trademarks

All terms mentioned in this book that are known to be trademarks or service marks have been appropriately capitalized. Neither THiNKaha, nor any of its imprints, can attest to the accuracy of this information. Use of a term in this book should not be regarded as affecting the validity of any trademark or service mark.

Warning and Disclaimer

Every effort has been made to make this book as complete and as accurate as possible. The information provided is on an "as is" basis. The author(s), publisher, and their agents assume no responsibility for errors or omissions. Nor do they assume liability or responsibility to any person or entity with respect to any loss or damages arising from the use of information contained herein.

Dedication

I dedicate this book to the two people that matter most. Me for writing it and you for reading it.

How to Read a THiNKaha® Book

A Note from the Publisher

The AHAthat/THiNKaha series was crafted to deliver content the way humans process information in today's world: short, sweet, and to the point while delivering powerful, lasting impact.

The content is designed and presented in ways to appeal to visual, auditory, and kinesthetic personality types. Each section contains AHA messages, lines for notes, and a meme that summarizes that section. You should also scan the QR code or click on the link to watch a video of the author talking about that section.

This book is contextual in nature. The words won't change, but every time you read them, their meaning and your context will. Be ready, because you will experience your own AHA moments as you read. The AHA messages are designed to be stand-alone actionable messages that will help you think differently. Items to consider as you're reading include the following:

1. It should take less than an hour to read the first time. When you're reading, write one to three action items that resonate with you in the underlined areas.
2. Mark your calendar to read it again.
3. Repeat step #1 and mark one to three additional AHA messages that resonate. As they will most likely be different, this is a great time to reflect on the messages that resonated with you during your last reading.
4. Sprinkle credust on both the author and yourself by sharing the AHA messages from this book socially from the AHAthat platform https://aha.pub/BestVersionOfYourself.

After reading this THiNKaha book, marking your AHA messages, re-reading it, and marking more AHA messages, you'll begin to see how this book contextually applies to you. As we advocate for continuous, lifelong learning, this book will help you transform your AHAs into action items with tangible results.

Mitchell Levy, Global Credibility Expert
publisher@thinkaha.com

THiNKaha®

A THiNKaha book is not your typical book. It's a whole lot more, while being a whole lot less. Scan the QR code or use this link to watch me talk about this new evolutionary style of book: https://aha.pub/THiNKahaSeries

Contents

Introduction

The world has dramatically changed. Real estate agents who want to succeed and thrive need to adapt and learn to handle sales more effectively without losing their humanity.

As a salesperson, you must constantly bet on yourself, improve your skills, and hone your capabilities to have a lasting impact on your clients and colleagues.

You can realize your fullest potential as a human being and an exceptional REALTOR when you recognize who you are, what you are passionate about, and how open you are to feedback and mentoring as your journey progresses in becoming the best that you can be.

There's a great deal of wisdom in maintaining a can-do attitude and a positive approach to real estate sales, and you can apply these lessons to your everyday life. To be a successful REALTOR, you need to surround yourself with people who support and encourage you.

How can you transition from being an average agent to an exceptional REALTOR? Real estate agents who are coachable, hungry, and comfortable in their own skin are the ones who stay on top of their game.

It's also essential to establish credibility by presenting yourself as someone whom prospective homebuyers and sellers can know, like, and trust.

This book shares valuable insights and life lessons for new REALTORS and longtime agents (who are humble enough to admit that they need to up their game) on how to be trusted, as well as credible real estate agents committed to providing outstanding service to their clients. It also enlightens salespeople on the impact that they can have with their networks and circles of influence as they become the best versions of themselves that they can possibly be.

Becoming a successful salesperson takes time, effort, and energy. There will be sleepless nights, blood, sweat, and tears -- literally and figuratively. What's winning worth to you? #RealtorSuccess

Kyle Seyboth

https://aha.pub/BestVersionOfYourself

Share the AHA messages from this book socially by going to
https://aha.pub/BestVersionOfYourself

Scan the QR code or use this link to watch the section videos and more on this section topic:
https://aha.pub/BestVersionOfYourselfSVs

Section I

Introduction

Many real estate agents are full of themselves and think they know everything. Either they have become so complacent that they're fine with whatever stereotyped impression society has of them, or they are too lazy to work to get things done and get them right.

Knowing their purpose—why they're doing what they do—is a characteristic that any good REALTOR should possess. Once they establish this, they will better understand their prospects' needs and be able to serve them with credibility.

Selling should be done purposefully to help homebuyers and sellers achieve their goals. This means experiencing a paradigm shift—seeing things with a fresh perspective—in overcoming challenges and always presenting your best self to your prospects.

Are you ready to do what it takes to be a successful REALTOR? Learn what drives you, adapt to changes, and never settle for "just enough" as you constantly improve your trade.

Additionally, it is more fulfilling to do business when you're not only growing your own career but also genuinely helping other people—clients and colleagues—along the way.

This section provides the premise for the entire book: how Realtors can be the best versions of themselves by utilizing their strengths and capabilities—mental, emotional, and physical—as guiding principles toward success.

1

Achieving #RealtorSuccess is possible. You have all the capabilities to be successful, both in life and in business, within you.

_____

_____

_____

2

When you make the most of the talents and skills that you were blessed with, you can achieve #RealtorSuccess.

_____

_____

_____

3

Eagerness, coachability, attentiveness, and confidence in one's ability -- these are key factors to #RealtorSuccess.

_____

_____

_____

4

A good salesperson has both style and substance; it isn't just smoke and mirrors. #RealtorSuccess

_____

_____

_____

5

A good REALTOR is someone who understands and gets to know people. Putting this understanding into action will determine your success with clients. #RealtorSuccess

_____

_____

6

Knowledge about sales and real estate comes easy. The key to success is putting it to good use. #RealtorSuccess

_____

_____

_____

7

Successful REALTORS are those who always have their clients' best interests at heart. #RealtorSuccess can be achieved when you use your abilities to help, understand, and meet people's needs.

_____

_____

_____

8

Too many salespeople try to fit clients into a one-size-fits-all formula. If you want to be a successful REALTOR, you need to know to avoid this pitfall. #RealtorSuccess

_____

_____

_____

9

Real estate is an asset, and as an agent, you're selling the asset, not just the property. What is the value proposition, and how does it benefit the client? #RealtorSuccess

_____

_____

_____

10

Intuition is born out of experience. Paying attention keeps it finely tuned and gives you an edge in understanding what your clients really need. #RealtorSuccess

_____

_____

_____

11

Is the service that you provide worth your clients'
precious time and money? 10 out of 10 times, you want
the answer to that question to be "yes." #RealtorSuccess

_____

_____

_____

12

"Laziness" is not a word that you'll find in an effective
salesperson's dictionary. If you're serious about
achieving #RealtorSuccess, do the work and commit to
the hustle.

_____

_____

_____

13

Never settle for mediocrity. Like the greats in any sport, you must give your all to realize success. #RealtorSuccess

_____

_____

_____

14

A successful REALTOR knows that the ultimate reward of putting in hours of work lies in the fulfillment that comes from helping people. #RealtorSuccess

_____

_____

_____

15

Becoming a successful salesperson takes time, effort, and energy. There will be sleepless nights, blood, sweat, and tears -- literally and figuratively. What's winning worth to you? #RealtorSuccess

_____

_____

_____

The most successful businesspeople are the ones who are truly themselves. You should work every day to become the best version of yourself.
#RealtorSuccess

Kyle Seyboth

https://aha.pub/BestVersionOfYourself

Share the AHA messages from this book socially by going to
https://aha.pub/BestVersionOfYourself

Scan the QR code or use this link to watch the section videos and more on this section topic:
https://aha.pub/BestVersionOfYourselfSVs

Section II

Be Yourself

In life and in any profession, there's no value in pretending to be someone you're not. This is especially true for real estate agents or anyone in the sales industry. Your clients will not believe in you if you're saying one thing and doing another. You must walk the walk and maintain integrity.

To achieve this, you must first know and embrace who you are and then prune anything unnecessary in your life and profession. You must be true to who you are and remain anchored by strong values and convictions.

Successful REALTORS are comfortable in their own skin after optimizing their lives for growth as a person. Being yourself and becoming a better salesperson means showing vulnerability and consistently learning and growing.

This section deals with how being real can be seen and felt by the people around you. By being genuine and true to yourself, you can be a successful REALTOR with whom prospects want to connect and do business.

16

People notice how you show up. Be genuine and true to who you are to be successful in your endeavors. #BeYourself #RealtorSuccess

_____

_____

_____

17

When you genuinely want to help, people can tell. It can be seen, heard, and felt. You can't fool anyone for long -- not even yourself. #BeYourself #RealtorSuccess

_____

_____

_____

18

You can truly make a difference in people's lives by
#BeingYourself. It really is that simple. #RealtorSuccess

_____

_____

_____

19

A good salesperson has a story to share and people to
help; they don't just deliver lines from a script.
Real is better than rehearsed. #RealtorSuccess

_____

_____

_____

20

A good REALTOR is passionate and real, and prospects can see that. Your story and the passion you carry will come out naturally. #BeYourself #RealtorSuccess

_____

_____

_____

21

If you're in a position to help your clients and your community, make a unique impact by being your unique self. There's only one you. #BeYourself #RealtorSuccess

_____

_____

_____

22

Don't worry -- feeling lost and not knowing yourself is often the first step to figuring out who you really are. #BeYourself #RealtorSuccess

_____

_____

_____

23

Are you struggling with who you really are? In making a change for the better, being lost is often a good place to start. Stay positive and keep an open mind. #BeYourself #RealtorSuccess

_____

_____

_____

24

Not knowing what to do or how to do it can open the door for vital self-assessment. #BeYourself #RealtorSuccess

_____

_____

_____

25

Figure out who you are and what makes you tick. One good measure of #RealtorSuccess is being comfortable in your own skin. #BeYourself

_____

_____

_____

26

When you're doing something you love, the realness comes through; your prospects will see and appreciate it and want to be around you. #BeYourself #RealtorSuccess

_____

_____

_____

27

In real estate sales, you want to be someone with whom your clients can relate. Share what you know and be vulnerable enough to admit what you don't know. #BeYourself #RealtorSuccess

_____

_____

_____

28

Being relatable means being someone whom your prospects can trust. Stay real and walk the walk. #BeYourself #RealtorSuccess

_____

_____

_____

Being the Best Version of Yourself

31

29

It's in everyone's best interest to say what you mean and mean what you say. No one gets away with fooling people for long. #BeYourself #RealtorSuccess

30

Faking your way to success is no success at all. #RealtorSuccess #BeReal #BeYourself

31

In sales, as in life, success isn't just winning the big game at the end. Getting there is a process. Commit yourself to an ongoing learning process. #BeYourself #RealtorSuccess

_____

_____

_____

32

Some salespeople think that they know it all when they
should be striving to learn. Keep listening, and always
stay true to your core self. #BeYourself #RealtorSuccess

_____

_____

_____

33

Clients are drawn to you when you stick to your core
values instead of copying what others are doing.
#RealtorSuccess

_____

_____

_____

34

Constant self-improvement is a primary goal of any successful salesperson. #BeingYourself doesn't mean being set in your ways. #RealtorSuccess

_____

_____

_____

35

A good REALTOR is constantly striving to become a better salesperson, colleague, and human. Adaptation is the key to making positive changes. #BeYourself #RealtorSuccess

_____

_____

_____

36

A good idea from fresh eyes and a new perspective can turn into success if you listen. #BeYourself #RealtorSuccess

_____

_____

_____

37

The real win in real estate sales is improving yourself, solving your clients' problems, and constantly growing along the way. Do that, and the money usually takes care of itself. #BeYourself #RealtorSuccess

_____

_____

_____

38

A successful REALTOR knows when to make amends and when to pull the plug. Maintaining good relationships with your clients and being true to yourself is always a win. #BeYourself #RealtorSuccess

_____

_____

_____

39

When you're true to yourself, people will love or hate you, but seeing your authenticity helps them know you, like you, and want to work with you. #BeYourself #RealtorSuccess

---

40

The most successful businesspeople are the ones who are truly themselves. You should work every day to become the best version of yourself. #RealtorSuccess

---

Ignite the hunger within once again. Sometimes it takes a mentor to spark the inspiration that will reignite and skyrocket your #RealtorSuccess. #BeHungry

Kyle Seyboth
https://aha.pub/BestVersionOfYourself

Share the AHA messages from this book socially by going to
https://aha.pub/BestVersionOfYourself

Scan the QR code or use this link to watch the section videos and more on this section topic:
https://aha.pub/BestVersionOfYourselfSVs

Section III

Be Hungry

Have you ever wanted something so much that you'd never give up—no matter what adversities came your way? That's passion. That's what it means to be hungry.

In real estate, competition can be difficult. But because you understand who you are and you strive to be better, you know that your only real competition is yourself. In fact, this mindset shows that if you are passionate enough to achieve your personal and financial goals, you can easily transition from striving to thriving.

You will find yourself thriving as a salesperson when you love what you're doing. How badly do you want to be a successful REALTOR? That fire in your belly will help you find your way and establish a clear plan to become the best you can be.

In this section, both new and longtime REALTORS can learn and rediscover their passion for providing excellent service in the real estate industry. These lessons can also be applied in life, and they include how you can stay motivated and inspired in fulfilling your goals and dreams.

41

Success requires effort. Success requires motivation. Success requires drive. #BeHungry for #RealtorSuccess.

_____

_____

_____

42

Your passion is your hunger for more. Seek it, and you'll achieve #RealtorSuccess in no time. #BeHungry

_____

_____

_____

43

To #BeHungry in real estate is to have that fire in your belly. Let it burn. #RealtorSuccess.

_____

_____

_____

44

Once you arrive at the peak of your career, your hunger and desire to be the best in your field will only increase your determination to stay number one. #RealtorSuccess

_____

_____

_____

45

Know what you're good at and #BeHungry for further self-development. #RealtorSuccess

_____

_____

_____

46

#BeHungry not only for financial success but also for knowledge and building better relationships. #RealtorSuccess

_____

_____

_____

47

Real estate is like running a marathon. You need to have fire in your belly to win against the competition. #BeHungry #RealtorSuccess

----

48

Discovering your best talents helps make you determined to improve yourself. #BeHungry #RealtorSuccess

----

49

Always #BeHungry for learning. Invest in your education so you can be a top REALTOR. #RealtorSuccess

_____

_____

_____

50

At some point, you lose your passion for becoming a top sales agent. But you can reignite this fire by rediscovering what made you strive for it in the first place. #BeHungry #StayHungry #RealtorSuccess

_____

_____

_____

51

Some REALTORS have buyers and sellers lining up at their door, while others don't. If you're not in abundance, are you learning from those who can help? #BeHungry #LearnMore

---

52

Ignite the hunger within once again. Sometimes it takes a mentor to spark the inspiration that will reignite and skyrocket your #RealtorSuccess. #BeHungry

---

53

Adversity is your friend -- always remember that.
Once you've won against its raging fire, you'll come out
stronger and wiser than ever. #RealtorSuccess

_____

_____

_____

54

Life is a game of sports. So what if you missed a few
shots? Just keep shooting. #BeHungry #RealtorSuccess

_____

_____

_____

55

Set lofty goals and work hard to achieve them. These goals will help you #BeHungry and produce results you will be proud of. #RealtorSuccess

_____

_____

_____

56

Most people dread Mondays. But when you love your work, no Monday could ever be dreadful! #BeHungry #RealtorSuccess

_____

_____

_____

57

Do you know what your "best self" is? It's a version of yourself that has the fire to #BeHungry to pursue #RealtorSuccess.

_____

_____

_____

58

Pursue what you want with a vengeance.
Nothing happens overnight, but your aspirations will lead you to success. #BeHungry #RealtorSuccess

_____

_____

_____

59

Be intentional in helping your clients, collaborators, and yourself experience all aspects of #RealtorSuccess.

_____

_____

_____

60

Be the best REALTOR possible. Give your clients what they want, when they want it, at each and every step. #BeHungry for #RealtorSuccess.

_____

_____

_____

#BeingCoachable means listening. When you listen, you learn and get a better understanding of the market and your clients. #RealtorSuccess

Kyle Seyboth

https://aha.pub/BestVersionOfYourself

Share the AHA messages from this book socially by going to
https://aha.pub/BestVersionOfYourself

Scan the QR code or use this link to watch the section videos and more on this section topic:
https://aha.pub/BestVersionOfYourselfSVs

Section IV

Be Coachable

There's nowhere to go but up for real estate agents who are willing to be coached and mentored.

Regardless of how long you've been in the business or how many units you have sold, there will always be:

· upcoming, rising REALTORS
· more knowledgeable prospects
· new strategies and technologies in the real estate market

Having the humility to accept that you need someone with more experience and knowledge to learn from is a good demonstration of coachability. Counsel can come from unexpected people and situations. If you're open to correction and wisdom, you are always in a position to skyrocket your success.

This section tackles how real estate agents can be receptive to constructive feedback and instruction from trusted advisors, colleagues, mentors, and peers. This section focuses on the benefits of being coachable, which can keep you trained, pushed, disciplined, and challenged to reach new heights in your personal and professional life.

61

Being the best version of yourself includes #BeingCoachable for the rest of your life. It's not about comparing yourself to others, but comparing yourself today with who you were yesterday. #RealtorSuccess

_____

_____

_____

62

There's always an opportunity to learn and grow. If you don't think that's true, you won't be seen as credible. #BeCoachable #RealtorSuccess

_____

_____

_____

63

Real estate sales are constantly evolving. #BeingCoachable enables you to adapt. #RealtorSuccess

_____

_____

_____

64

Coachability means different things to different people. Ultimately, the goal is to use feedback to improve. #BeCoachable #RealtorSuccess

_____

_____

_____

65

Keep your eyes and ears open so you can learn a thing
or two from everyone you meet. #BeingCoachable
#RealtorSuccess

_____

_____

_____

66

Learn lessons and acquire habits from others and
make it your goal to adopt what works for you.
#BeingCoachable #RealtorSuccess

_____

_____

_____

67

#BeingCoachable means listening. When you listen, you learn and get a better understanding of the market and your clients. #RealtorSuccess

---

68

Thinking that you know it all is the first sign that you have much more to learn. #BeCoachable #RealtorSuccess

---

69

Not everything requires an immediate response.
You can make better decisions when you take the time
to digest what you've learned and how to apply it.
#BeCoachable #RealtorSuccess

_____

_____

_____

70

A reaction is impulsive and often lacks the clarity of
thought that can be levied with a well-considered
response. #BeCoachable #RealtorSuccess

_____

_____

_____

71

You perform at the level of those around you. Seek collaborators and mentors with more experience than you and soak up their expertise. #BeCoachable #RealtorSuccess

_____

_____

_____

72

What makes someone great? Dissect what "great" people do, even outside your industry. Take inspiration, habits, and mentalities from the greats, and make them your own. #BeCoachable #RealtorSuccess

_____

_____

_____

73

It doesn't matter how much natural talent you have or how much hard work you put in. Every All-Star and MVP reaches their potential with the help of coaching. #BeCoachable #RealtorSuccess

_____

_____

_____

74

Even Tiger Woods worked with coaches and trainers before he made it big, and guess what? After making it big, he still works with coaches to learn new things. It never stops. #BeCoachable #RealtorSuccess

_____

_____

_____

75

It's no coincidence that Michael Jordan and Kobe Bryant -- two of the greatest of all time -- shared the same coach. Find your Phil Jackson. #BeCoachable #RealtorSuccess

---

76

There is no such thing as "perfecting the craft." Fall in love with the process of perpetual improvement. #BeCoachable #RealtorSuccess

---

77

No one likes a salesperson with a big ego.
#BeingCoachable keeps you humble. It's cool to
be humble. Being humble is good for business.
#RealtorSuccess

_____

_____

_____

78

You can learn from anyone at any age. Old dogs can
learn new tricks, and young pups can learn from the
wisdom of experience. #BeCoachable #RealtorSuccess

_____

_____

_____

79

Be open-minded. You can always learn from discussions with colleagues and clients. Talking through it helps. #BeCoachable #RealtorSuccess

---

80

People have different styles, methods, and ways of going about things. You'd be surprised what you can learn with an open mind. #BeCoachable #RealtorSuccess

---

81

There is no need to take offense when someone shares their insights with you. That's ego BS. Be secure enough to take the good and dispense with the bad. #BeCoachable #RealtorSuccess

---

82

There are always ways to improve and elements to add to your arsenal. What's one area of your business where you could make improvements? Who might be a good coaching resource? #BeCoachable #RealtorSuccess

---

83

Make a habit of taking advice and trying new things based on good ideas from mentors and collaborators. Maximizing adaptability is a superpower. #BeCoachable #RealtorSuccess

_____

_____

_____

84

Having the humility and enthusiasm to hear ideas from others can open doors and create opportunities for dialogue and future collaboration. #BeCoachable #RealtorSuccess

_____

_____

_____

85

Coachability leads to credibility. Clients should have confidence doing business with someone who listens and is coachable. #BeCoachable #RealtorSuccess

_____

_____

_____

Growth is finding something within yourself as a direct result of failure. Recognizing what you failed to accomplish -- and why -- is vital to learning.
#RealtorSuccess

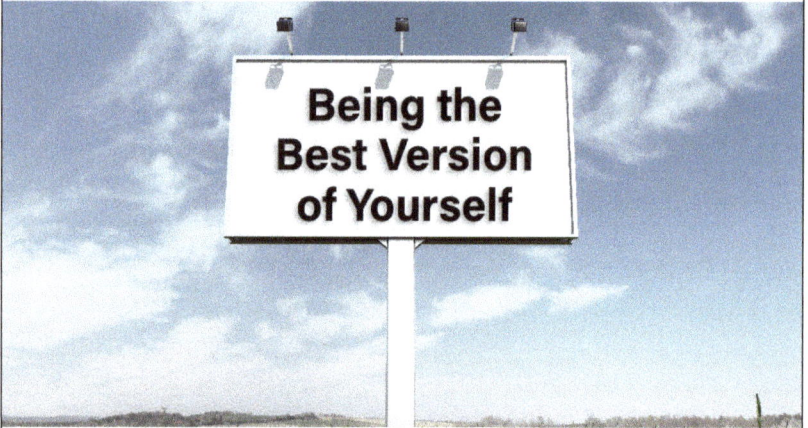

Being the Best Version of Yourself

Kyle Seyboth

https://aha.pub/BestVersionOfYourself

Share the AHA messages from this book socially by going to
https://aha.pub/BestVersionOfYourself

Scan the QR code or use this link to watch the section videos and more on this section topic:
https://aha.pub/BestVersionOfYourselfSVs

Section V

Find Your Lane and Stay There

In a competitive environment, you can't help getting affected by myriad stimuli as you go about your business. As a salesperson, it's important to find your lane and stay there in order to develop habits that will make you an expert in your chosen profession.

Staying in your lane means becoming an expert in a specific area. You have your flow, and you constantly get better in that area.

The metaphor of life being a highway can be applied to real estate selling. No matter what speed bumps or roadblocks you encounter, you can stay focused when you begin with the end in mind.

This section is for REALTORS who may or may not have found their lanes yet. They should know who they are, understand their value, and work within a conducive space to establish their credibility. This will give them a better chance at becoming successful real estate agents who consistently create a positive impact in the community.

86

Good REALTORS stay in their own lane, keep moving forward, and don't crowd other lanes. #RealtorSuccess

_____

_____

_____

87

Perhaps you've found your lane; perhaps not. For legitimate #RealtorSuccess, find something that gets you excited and then own it.

_____

_____

_____

88

Don't be afraid to try different things to find your lane.
It rarely happens on the first try. #RealtorSuccess

_____

_____

_____

89

Failing forward is failing in a way that results in learning,
gaining experience, and bettering yourself. That's how
you find your lane to begin with. #RealtorSuccess

_____

_____

_____

90

Growth is finding something within yourself as a direct result of failure. Recognizing what you failed to accomplish -- and why -- is vital to learning. #RealtorSuccess

_____

_____

_____

91

Finding your lane means it's all that you think about morning and night. Where does YOUR mind go? #RealtorSuccess

_____

_____

_____

92

To achieve #RealtorSuccess, explore the market, understand the industry, and learn about your customers. Soon, you'll be able to pin down your niche. #BeHungry

---

93

In real life, you wouldn't suddenly change lanes on a five-lane highway. You'll reach your goals faster when you stay in your lane. #RealtorSuccess

---

94

Life is a highway. Once you find your lane, put the pedal down and go. You'll see how effortless your work becomes once you're in the flow. #RealtorSuccess

_____

_____

_____

95

To be a successful REALTOR, stay in your lane by specializing at a high level while maintaining integrity, humility, and credibility. Doing so will set you apart from subpar agents. #RealtorSuccess

_____

_____

_____

96

To enhance what you're really good at, you can try something new, fail, and try again while staying in your lane. This is the road to opportunity. #RealtorSuccess

_____

_____

_____

97

Understand your lane and why you're there. When you're true to yourself while doing what you love, you leave an impact while reaching your goals in the right way. #RealtorSuccess

_____

_____

_____

98

Finding your lane means being at the center of the action without being immersed in it. #RealtorSuccess

---

99

Through repetition and experience, you develop expertise. Sharing it with heart and gratitude makes you a credible, trusted resource in your field. #RealtorSuccess

---

100

It's better to do one thing well than many things with inconsistent results. Find one thing that you're good at, and stay in your lane. #RealtorSuccess

_____

_____

_____

101

Follow the path inside you, not the path that you're "supposed" to be on. That could lead to mediocrity. Stay in your lane intentionally. #RealtorSuccess

_____

_____

_____

102

To be a successful agent, focus on the income-generating activities of the sales business. Some people mistakenly think that their lane is wider than it really is. #RealtorSuccess

---

103

Becoming a specialist is one of the benefits of staying in your lane. You'll never become great at something if you keep changing lanes. #RealtorSuccess

---

104

Understand your value and credibility. Know who and what you are. This will help you stay in your lane. #RealtorSuccess

_____

_____

_____

105

The beauty of finding your lane -- and staying there -- is that you get to invest yourself in a specific forte without getting derailed from your long-term goals. #RealtorSuccess

_____

_____

_____

106

You gotta be "in the flow" and "go with the flow" -- that's how you find your lane and stay in it. #RealtorSuccess

_____

_____

_____

107

Going through life without finding what you love to do is a tragedy. The drive to succeed can propel you to great heights and prosperity. #BeHungry #RealtorSuccess

_____

_____

_____

108

You'll be surprised at the options that you'll have to ramp up your skills and connections once you're in the flow. Staying in your lane gives you a better chance of traveling on a bigger highway. #RealtorSuccess

_____

_____

_____

Spend your time around like-minded people who want to improve; this will help get you where you want to be. #RightPeople #RealtorSuccess

Kyle Seyboth

https://aha.pub/BestVersionOfYourself

Share the AHA messages from this book socially by going to
https://aha.pub/BestVersionOfYourself

Scan the QR code or use this link to watch the section videos and more on this section topic:
https://aha.pub/BestVersionOfYourselfSVs

Section VI

Surround Yourself With the Right People and Right Attitude

It's easy to focus on naysayers and want to prove them wrong, but in real estate selling, it's better to focus on your supporters and prove to them that you're worth supporting.

What does this mean? When you pay attention to what helps you become better, you are more inclined to succeed. You are inspired to go to the next level when you surround yourself with people who want what's best for you. By and large, it means dialing in on the positive more than on the negative.

This is an interesting shift on what real estate agents should be listening to without necessarily shutting down negative feedback, which also has value. It simply means that you attract what you are ready for. When you believe right, you live and act right.

Do your critics mean to put you down, or are they actually rooting for your success? Anything that encourages you to produce positive outcomes helps you become a better person and an exceptional REALTOR.

This section explores what REALTORS should be dedicating their time to, which influences what they think, act on, and believe in. Surround yourself with the right people who support you, and you will set yourself up to achieve beyond your expectations.

109

Surround yourself with positive people who support and encourage you to thrive as your best self. #RightPeople #RightAttitude #RealtorSuccess

_____

_____

_____

110

Jettison anything in your life that brings you down. Focus on connecting with people who have similar goals, aspirations, and work ethics. #RightPeople #RealtorSuccess

_____

_____

_____

111

Your circle of influence should be a place where you can listen to good counsel. These are the people who sometimes believe in you more than you believe in yourself. #RightPeople #RealtorSuccess

_____

_____

_____

112

In real estate, you need to be aware of who influences what you believe, say, and do. Whose voice are you listening to? #RightPeople #RealtorSuccess

_____

_____

_____

113

Spend your time around like-minded people who want to improve; this will help get you to where you want to be. #RightPeople #RealtorSuccess

_____

_____

_____

114

Everyone has someone they listen to and who pushes them to be better. It's vital to surround yourself with people who help you become better. #RightPeople #RealtorSuccess

_____

_____

_____

115

Appreciate and take care of the people in your life. They see you for who you truly are. #RightPeople #RealtorSuccess

_____

_____

_____

116

Your accomplishments and #RealtorSuccess are not your own. They are the product of the support that you receive from your family, colleagues, mentors, and clients. Celebrate your wins and acknowledge those rooting for you. #RightPeople

_____

_____

_____

117

Any passion for proving your critics wrong should be put toward surrounding yourself with the right people. Give your attention to what builds you up rather than what brings you down. #RightPeople #RealtorSuccess

_____

_____

_____

118

Set your goals and go after them. Your critics might even become your supporters when they witness your integrity and credibility. #RightPeople #RealtorSuccess

_____

_____

_____

119

A positive mentality results in positive outcomes, just as a negative mentality results in negative outcomes. It all comes down to what you focus on. #RightAttitude #RealtorSuccess

_____

_____

_____

120

Positivity begets positivity. When your message is positive, your focus shifts from pointing out faults to proving people right. #RightAttitude #RealtorSuccess

_____

_____

_____

121

Real estate is bigger than any one person. Support and enable others in the business, just as you've been supported by others. #RightAttitude #RealtorSuccess

_____

_____

_____

122

A positive mindset creates positive energy around you. With a healthy lifestyle and the right mentality, your positivity can be contagious to those around you. #RightAttitude #RealtorSuccess

_____

_____

_____

123

Don't forget that the person who appreciates you the most is yourself. You are your biggest supporter. #RightAttitude #RealtorSuccess

_____

_____

_____

124

You get what you give. You receive support through generosity. See who needs help and lift others up. #RightAttitude #RealtorSuccess

_____

_____

_____

125

If you're looking to attract others to you, it's better to be the positive one among your peers vs. the negative one. #RightAttitude #RealtorSuccess

_____

_____

_____

126

Feed your mind, body, and soul whatever is good, noble, and pure. This is a key factor in achieving #RightAttitude #RealtorSuccess.

_____

_____

_____

127

In the face of a challenging task, it's always better to say, "I get to," rather than, "I have to." #RightAttitude #RealtorSuccess

_____

_____

_____

128

You asked for an opportunity. Show that it's a privilege to be here. #RightAttitude #RealtorSuccess

_____

_____

_____

129

If you come prepared and optimistic, you will see great results. How contagious is your energy? The energy around you is often a product of the energy you're putting out into the world. #RightAttitude #RealtorSuccess

_____

_____

_____

130

Start believing that the universe wants you to succeed rather than fail. You need to attract #RealtorSuccess to you in order to achieve it.

_____

_____

_____

Gamble on yourself -- you know what you're capable of. Take risks, invest in yourself, and spend money to make money. #PlayBig #RealtorSuccess

Kyle Seyboth

https://aha.pub/BestVersionOfYourself

Share the AHA messages from this book socially by going to
https://aha.pub/BestVersionOfYourself

Scan the QR code or use this link to watch the section videos and more on this section topic:
https://aha.pub/BestVersionOfYourselfSVs

Section VII

Play Big

A successful REALTOR plays big in the real estate market and in life.

Success is not necessarily quantified by the number of prospects you've talked to, buyers you've signed contracts with, houses you've sold, or accolades you've received.

The results of your perseverance and hard work will speak for themselves. However, living a truthful and inspirational life as a credible, authentic, and trusted real estate agent, one who genuinely takes the time to get to know prospects and provide solutions for their needs, is something that cannot be measured.

This is what it means to play big. You are not merely content with where you are and what you have done but are constantly improving and outperforming yourself to provide quality service to your clients. You always give 100% in all that you do.

This section concludes by reinforcing that a successful REALTOR'S ultimate win is not limited to tangible accomplishments. Build something bigger than yourself, and you will set the stage for bigger opportunities—not only for yourself, but also for other people around you.

131

The sky is the limit. Once you've found your niche, you can perform well and find happiness with every decision you make. #PlayBig #RealtorSuccess

_____

_____

_____

132

The whole is always greater than the sum of its parts. Regardless of your sales numbers, you are building something bigger than yourself. #PlayBig #RealtorSuccess

_____

_____

_____

133

For an agent, success doesn't come with a universal metric. It's not always measured on a scoreboard. #PlayBig #RealtorSuccess

_____

_____

_____

134

A stellar agent's ultimate goal is to be successful and fulfilled, no longer bound or defined by anyone's metrics but their own. #PlayBig #RealtorSuccess

_____

_____

_____

135

Gamble on yourself -- you know what you're capable of.
Take risks, invest in yourself, and spend money to make
money. #PlayBig #RealtorSuccess

_____

_____

_____

136

Leave behind others' preconceived notions of who you are and where you should be. The world is yours for the taking. #PlayBig #RealtorSuccess

_____

_____

_____

137

How badly do you want to achieve your goals? Are you willing to play as big as necessary? The time and energy you put into your work is a testament to your desire to make things happen. #PlayBig #RealtorSuccess

_____

_____

_____

138

#PlayingBig means many things, including serving clients in ways that involve sustainable solutions and long-term results, not just money. #RealtorSuccess

_____

_____

_____

139

When you play big and love what you do, you will enjoy the fruits of your labor and experience exponential success. #PlayBig #RealtorSuccess

_____

_____

_____

140

A successful agent plays big. They see and think about the big picture and how they can turn something small into something bigger than themselves. #PlayBig #RealtorSuccess

_____

_____

_____

About the Author

Kyle Seyboth, a REALTOR for Century 21, is one of the most trusted and best-selling REALTORS in the Rhode Island area. He utilizes the latest technologies, market research, and business strategies to achieve and maintain success.

Kyle was the #1 REALTOR in the country for Keller Williams four times before accepting a new opportunity with Century 21 to become a multi-office regional broker while developing a coaching program exclusively designed to outline his methods for Century 21 agents across the nation.

His clients and colleagues know and love Kyle for his commitment, stellar reputation, and can-do attitude as an agent and mentor in the local residential and commercial real estate market.

Kyle was nominated as a Top 10 National Real Estate Producer by *The Wall Street Journal* and is consistently named as a top REALTOR nationwide, having sold 144 units with roughly $16 million in sales in 2014 and reaching more than $120 million for 509 units in 2018, all while setting new records year after year.

Kyle provides the right guidance and communication to homebuyers and sellers to make the buying and home-selling process as stress-free as possible.

He is a proud father of two beautiful girls, and he loves coaching their sports on the weekends.

THiNKaha has created AHAthat for you to share content from this book.

- ➲ Share each AHA message socially: **https://aha.pub/BestVersionOfYourself**
- ➲ Share additional content: **https://AHAthat.com**
- ➲ Info on authoring: **https://AHAthat.com/Author**

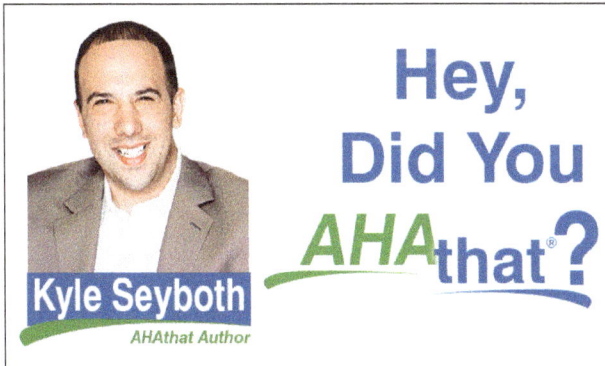

www.ingramcontent.com/pod-product-compliance
Lightning Source LLC
Chambersburg PA
CBHW042118190326
41519CB00030B/7542